THE ULTIMATE GUIDE TO YOUR INNER POWERPUFF AND QUIZ BOOK

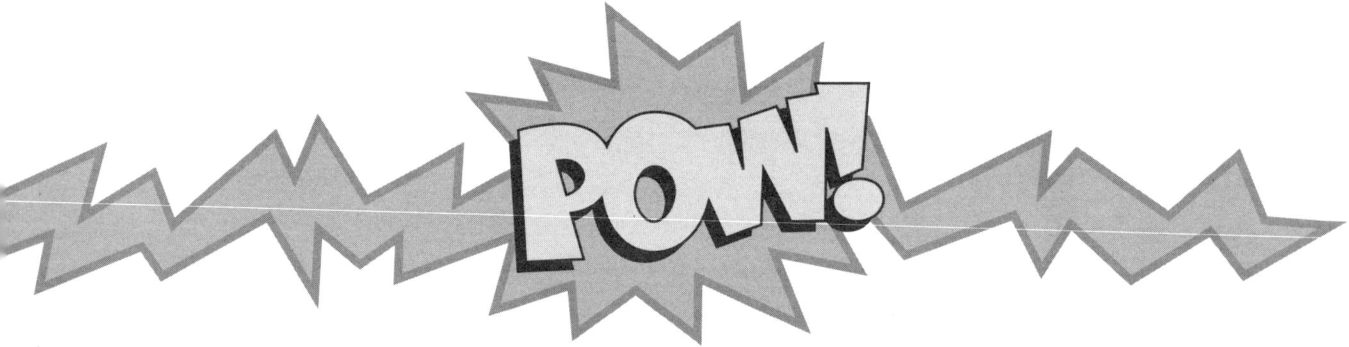
POW!

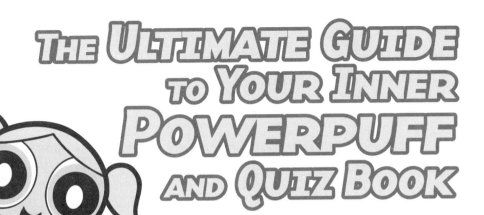

The ULTIMATE GUIDE to YOUR INNER POWERPUFF and QUIZ BOOK

by Amy Keating Rogers

Scholastic Inc.
New York · Toronto · London · Auckland · Sydney · Mexico City · New Delhi · Hong Kong · Buenos Aires

ISBN 0-439-33247-8

Designed by Mark Neston

12 11 10 9 8 7 6 5 4 3   2 3 4 5 6/0

Printed in U.S.A.

First Scholastic printing, January 2002

Table of Contents

I: Who Are The Powerpuff Girls?

The city of Townsville! A town protected by those pint-sized heroes, The Powerpuff Girls! Brainy Blossom, bubbly Bubbles, and brawny Buttercup make up this awesome threesome.

But just how did these super little girls come to be? Well, when Professor Utonium was trying to create the perfect little girl, he added together sugar, spice, and everything nice. But when his troublesome (and clumsy!) lab assistant monkey, Jojo, accidentally pushed the Professor into a container of Chemical X,

SUGAR

CHEMICAL X

1

BOOM!

it exploded, spilling some of this potent potion into that little-girl mix.

When Professor Utonium awoke from the blast, he saw not one but three perfect little girls. And not only were they perfect, they were super! That Chemical X really packed a punch. The Girls had laser eyes, super-strength (complete with power kicks and jabs), and the ability to fly. You name it, the Girls have it!

Since their creation, The Powerpuff Girls have used their powers for good, dedicating their lives to fighting crime and stopping the forces of evil—that is, when they're not attending their classes at Pokey Oaks Kindergarten!

And that's no mean feat in the city of Townsville. It may *look* like your average, happy city, full of pleasant people living their daily lives, but this place is just crawling with nasty no-gooders and terrible tyrants. The Girls are constantly having to save their city from a host of baddies. What follows is a rundown of them.

MOJO JOJO—A mutated monkey with an incredibly large brain that he uses to hatch his evil plots.

HIM—The ultimate evil, in a red, pointy-eared, lobster-clawed package. In fact, Him is so evil, you can't even say his real name!

BIG BILLY

SNAKE

THE GANGREEN GANG—A pack of hoodlums with a sickly green skin color. These guys are mainly pranksters, not really in the big leagues with Mojo and Him. The members of the Gangreen Gang are Ace (the leader), Snake, Grubber, Little Arturo, and Big Billy.

ACE

LITTLE ARTURO

GRUBBER

4

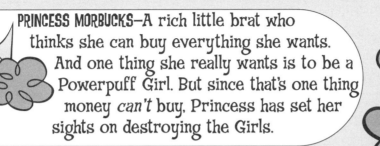

PRINCESS MORBUCKS—A rich little brat who thinks she can buy everything she wants. And one thing she really wants is to be a Powerpuff Girl. But since that's one thing money *can't* buy, Princess has set her sights on destroying the Girls.

FUZZY LUMPKINS—A hotheaded backwoods bully who hates it when anyone steps on his property.

THE AMOEBA BOYS—The worst criminals in Townsville. In other words, they're just terrible at committing crime. As hard as they try, these single-celled organisms aren't fully evolved enough to do anything evil!

SEDUSA—This nasty woman likes to disguise herself as a good, kind lady so she can fool kindhearted folks and steal from Townsville. She's got such dreadful locks of hair that even the Girls get all tied up in knots.

And that's not all! There's also an endless supply of monsters who come to terrorize Townsville. The Girls have their work cut out for them!

6

AND NOW, IT'S TIME TO MEET THE SUPERPOWERED TRIO!

BLOSSOM—A natural-born leader, Blossom has been the head of The Powerpuff Girls since the day they were created. Blossom is known for her organizational skills and her well-thought out plans. She's also the rational one. Some would consider her bossy, but really she just knows how to get the job done and does it! She loves to read, study, and learn. That's part of the everything nice that is central to being Blossom. She's also got her sugary side—this little girl enjoys a good game of hopscotch, going to the beach, and playing pretend with her sisters. And she has enough spice to be one mean fighter, ready to beat some sense into the bad guys of Townsville whenever necessary. Plus, Blossom's got ice breath, which her sisters don't.

BUTTERCUP—A tough fighter, a tough talker, and one tough cookie. Buttercup would like to be the leader of The Powerpuff Girls instead of Blossom, but her hotheaded ways often get her in trouble. Buttercup's motto is "Hit first, ask questions never," and she lives up to it. Buttercup is all action, even during playtime. When Buttercup plays, she plays to win. Still, she has been known to have a softer side. In fact, Buttercup can even be cute! This Girl has a little sugar and everything nice, but is chock-full of spice, and she will always give the bad guys a good lickin'!

BUBBLES—A sweetie with a heart of gold. Bubbles loves sunshine and rainbows, flowers and butterflies. She also loves to color pretty drawings of all the beautiful things in the world. Really, Bubbles loves everyone and everything—except anybody who's mean and nasty. That's when Bubbles goes hard-core, showing those baddies that she's no softy. Definitely the most full of sugar of the three sisters, Bubbles also has plenty of everything nice and just enough spice to make things interesting.

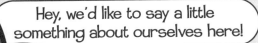

Hey, we'd like to say a little something about ourselves here!

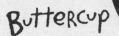

Buttercup

Yeah, this book is supposed to be all about us, so *we* should do the talking!

Blossom

We're super talkers!

Bubbles

Hello! This is Blossom of The Powerpuff Girls. My sisters, Bubbles and Buttercup, and I want to personally welcome you to **The Ultimate Guide to Your Inner Powerpuff and Quiz Book.** Some of you will already know us really well. But for others, this may be the first time we've ever met. So hi-glad to meet you. In this book, you're going to find out which one of us you're most like.

Blah, blah, blah. That's all the mushy stuff. Tell them the other good stuff!

9

I was getting to it, but if you're in such a hurry, why don't you tell them yourself, Buttercup?

Fine, I will. Hi, everybody. Buttercup here. Sorry Blossom was jabbering so much. The other cool thing about this book is that there's also a bunch of quizzes in here about all the adventures we've had as The Powerpuff Girls, so you can test your Powerpuff Girl IQ!

Wait! I want to say something, too!

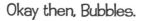

Okay then, Bubbles.

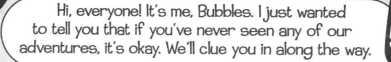

Hi, everyone! It's me, Bubbles. I just wanted to tell you that if you've never seen any of our adventures, it's okay. We'll clue you in along the way.

Good point, Bubbles. Now, Buttercup thinks this Inner Powerpuff stuff is mushy, but I think it's really cool. You see, everyone has the ability of a Powerpuff inside them, even if you weren't born with superpowers. So we're here to guide you toward the Powerpuff you're most like. Are you a leader like me? Are you strong and tough like Buttercup? Are you soft and sweet like Bubbles? Or are you a combination of the three of us—sometimes in charge, other times tough, but always a little sweet?

In this book, you'll find out what your combination of sugar, spice, and everything nice is. And even if you aren't a hero with superpowers to fight crime and bad guys, it's still good to find out your inner Powerpuff. There's a lot of wrong in the world, and by using your inner Powerpuff, you can help make it better.

If you're a leader like me, you can help organize ways to make your school or neighborhood a better place. If you're strong like Buttercup, you can make sure that if people are being hurt, someone is going to be there to help them. And if you're sweet like Bubbles, you can make the world a more beautiful place by having a positive attitude. So if everybody is ready...

12

WHICH POWERPUFF IS YOUR STUFF?

Hi! My sisters and I have been in a bunch of situations and we're here to look at the different ways we each reacted to them. For each scenario below, circle the answer that's most like you. Or pick the answer that describes how you would've reacted to the same situation if you were a Powerpuff Girl—or if you were a villain.

Once you're done, here's how to score your quiz: Every question has an answer that fits what I would do, what Buttercup would do, what Bubbles would do, and what a villain would do in each situation. So when you're done checking out all the answers you'll have a Blossom score, a Buttercup score, a Bubbles score, and a villain score. Which is the highest? Or do you have a little bit of all of us in you? I sure hope you haven't got too much villain in you—if you do, you'd better watch out for The Powerpuff Girls!

Blossom

13

1. Mojo Jojo is destroying Townsville! You

   a. Use Powerpuff Plan A-3 to stop that meddlesome monkey.
   b. Think, "Oh, what a cute, sad monkey," and then attack him.
   c. Hit that Mojo square in the jaw, no questions asked.
   d. Let him destroy Townsville and rule the world!

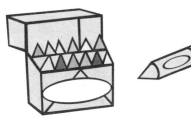

2. The villain Mr. Mime has turned Townsville black and white! You

   a. Get out your crayons to bring the color back to Townsville.
   b. Look for clues to solve this colorless crime.
   c. Sit back and relax. Who cares if Townsville has no color?
   d. Hunt down every last drop of color and take it away.

3. What do you have more of?

    a. Sugar

    b. Spice

    c. Everything nice

    d. Tartar sauce

4. The Amoeba Boys are throwing trash in the street. You

    a. Giggle at those silly Amoeba Boys.

    b. Tell them to clean up after themselves before you get nasty.

    c. Warn them that if they play in the street, they could get hurt.

    d. Hope they keep it up.

5. It's time for fun at The Powerpuff Girls' house. You

    a. Get out the video games and start playing.

    b. Sit down with a good book and read.

    c. Play with Octi and all your other stuffed animals.

    d. Polish up your plan to finally destroy those meddlesome Girls!

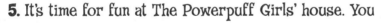

6. Hillbilly bad guy Fuzzy Lumpkins is shooting at squirrels! You

   a. Melt his boomstick with your laser eyes.

   b. Call the squirrels together by speaking their language.

   c. Toss that Fuzzy right in the slammer, where he belongs.

   d. Chase down anything that gets on your property.

7. Sedusa, the snaky-haired villainess, has kidnapped Ms. Keane, the Pokey Oaks teacher! You

   a. Organize The Powerpuff Girls for the perfect plan of attack.

   b. Take on that snake-haired hooligan.

   c. Find Ms. Keane and sing her a pretty, pretty song.

   d. Catch those brats right in your super locks of hair.

8. The Professor has made your favorite meal. It's

   a. Fish, a great brain food.

   b. Meat, a great power food.

   c. Ice cream, a great yummy food.

   d. Squirrel sandwiches, a great hillbilly food.

9. When Mojo Jojo reveals that he was once the Professor's lab monkey, Jojo, you

   a. Are stunned.

   b. Think he's a big liar.

   c. Are upset 'cause you could have had a pet monkey!

   d. Insist that the Professor give you the same powers that The Powerpuff Girls have.

10. Princess is trying to join The Powerpuff Girls again. You

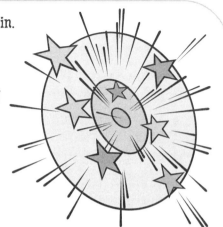

    a. Freeze her new super suit with your ice breath.

    b. Try to explain that to be a Powerpuff she really needs some "everything nice."

    c. Show that brat what real Powerpuffs are made of.

    d. Yell at your Daddy to give you more money, so you can bribe your way into joining.

11. When The Powerpuff Girls play a pretend Powerpuff adventure on a rainy day, you

    a. Pretend to be a ferocious monster.

    b. Play yourself, 'cause you're so cute!

    c. Pretend to be Ms. Bellum, since she's the smartest.

    d. Are glad those Powerpuffs are not bugging you for once.

12. Your classmate Mitch Mitchelson has turned Twiggy, the class hamster, into a monster. You

  a. Do nothing. Twiggy will give that rotten Mitch just what he deserves.

  b. Try to talk to sweet Twiggy, who never meant to be a monster.

  c. Do something good for Twiggy by finding a giant wheel for him to chase Mitch in forever.

  d. Run as Twiggy chases after you.

13. Right before bedtime you

  a. Brush your hair one hundred times to make sure it's silky smooth.

  b. Clean up your crayons, making sure all the pretty colors are there.

  c. Stretch out, making sure your muscles are ready for tomorrow's hard-hitting day.

  d. Read *Villains Monthly* magazine.

14. A mean, nasty monster is attacking the city. You

    a. Attack him right back!

    b. Watch his every move to figure out how best to defeat the beast.

    c. Ask him very nicely to go home.

    d. Pick off those puny Powerpuffs one by one.

15. Ms. Keane is offering extra credit. You

    a. Run out to the playground and start playing.

    b. Get right to work on those extra credit points.

    c. Start drawing a nice new picture of a happy sun.

    d. Start a fight in the classroom.

16. When the Girls adopt a squirrel, you want to name it

    a. Bruce.

    b. Miss Fluffy.

    c. Lady Josephine.

    d. Mini Jojo.

17. When flying, you see the clouds as

    a. Clouds. Duh.

    b. Collections of the moisture in Earth's atmosphere.

    c. Horsies and bunnies and hearts.

    d. More annoying puffs you have to avoid.

18. Mojo Jojo has used a magic statue to turn everyone into dogs. You

    a. Are excited because now everyone is a puppy!

    b. Find a way to smash that statue.

    c. Give that monkey just what he deserves—a good bite on the behind.

    d. Know that your plan to take over the world will finally succeed!

19. Your classmate Elmer Sglue, angry at being teased for eating paste, has eaten radioactive glue and turned into a Paste Monster. You

    a. Say you're sorry for making fun of him.

    b. Feel sorry for Elmer, 'cause he's awfully nice.

    c. Demand that your sister say she's sorry for making fun of him.

    d. Make everyone stick like glue for making fun of you.

20. There's a cockroach in the house. You

    a. Scream like a scaredy-cat and beg someone to squish it.

    b. Try to get everyone to calm down. It may be gross, but it's just a bug.

    c. Chase after that stupid bug, trying to shoot it with your laser eyes.

    d. Scoop up the roach and scare people with it.

21. You're creating an imaginary friend. You make sure she

    a. Wears combat boots.

    b. Is a fluffy bunny.

    c. Is very intelligent.

    d. Wreaks havoc in the classroom.

22. Your creepy classmate Harry Pitt is trying to give you his cooties. You

    a. Know there are no such things as cooties and pay no attention to Harry.

    b. Run screaming from Harry in fear of the cooties.

    c. Tell Harry if he gets any closer, he'll get it right in the kisser.

    d. Use Harry as a shield to commit crime.

23. Big Billy of the Gangreen Gang has decided to be your friend and wait on you hand and foot. You

   a. Think it's great. You always wanted a butler.

   b. Are suspicious since any member of the Gangreen Gang can never be up to any good.

   c. Giggle as he brushes your hair.

   d. Don't even notice that Big Billy has left the Gangreen Gang to join The Powerpuff Girls.

24. The Professor is buying you a new toy. You have him get you

   a. A super science set.

   b. More stuffed animals.

   c. A catcher's mitt and baseball.

   d. A new "Ship in a Bottle" kit.

25. Abra Cadaver, the zombie magician, has risen from his grave to attack Townsville. You

   a. Hide under the couch cushions because zombies scare you.

   b. Get ready to fight him—you're not scared of any zombie!

   c. Show that zombie that you have special Powerpuff magic of your own.

   d. Zap the citizens with your evil magic.

BONUS QUESTION:

When it comes to working out a problem, you think it's best solved with

   a. Your mind.

   b. Your strength.

   c. Your charm.

   d. Your evil.

ANSWERS:

1. Mojo is always trying to destroy Townsville. But that menacing monkey never wins!

   a. Blossom b. Bubbles c. Buttercup d. villain

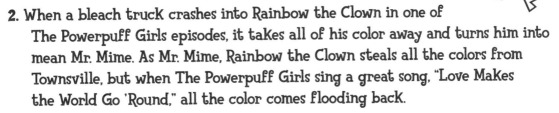

2. When a bleach truck crashes into Rainbow the Clown in one of The Powerpuff Girls episodes, it takes all of his color away and turns him into mean Mr. Mime. As Mr. Mime, Rainbow the Clown steals all the colors from Townsville, but when The Powerpuff Girls sing a great song, "Love Makes the World Go 'Round," all the color comes flooding back.

   a. Bubbles b. Blossom c. Buttercup d. villain

3. When the Professor combined sugar, spice, and everything nice to make the perfect little girl, Bubbles got the sugar, Buttercup got the spice, and Blossom got the everything nice—plus the Girls all got Chemical X!

   a. Bubbles b. Buttercup c. Blossom d. villain

4. The Amoeba Boys are always trying to commit crimes, but they're really not very good at it!

a. Bubbles b. Buttercup c. Blossom d. villain

5. After a hard day of crime fighting, each of the Girls does her own thing to unwind.

a. Buttercup b. Blossom c. Bubbles d. villain

6. Fuzzy Lumpkins isn't very nice and shoots at the squirrels that get on his property.

a. Buttercup b. Bubbles c. Blossom d. villain

7. Sedusa has never actually kidnapped Ms. Keane, but she did kidnap Ms. Bellum once.

a. Blossom b. Buttercup c. Bubbles d. villain

8. The Professor always tries to make The Powerpuff Girls their favorite foods.

a. Blossom b. Buttercup c. Bubbles d. villain

9. When the Girls find out that Mojo used to be the Professor's lab monkey, they can't believe it!

a. Blossom b. Buttercup c. Bubbles d. villain

10. Princess decided that she wants to be a Powerpuff Girl, but The Powerpuff Girls said no. She's been mad at them ever since!

a. Blossom b. Bubbles c. Buttercup d. villain

11. When it rains, even the villains stay home—so the Girls have no crime to fight. That's when Buttercup, Bubbles, and Blossom play pretend Powerpuff adventures instead.

a. Buttercup b. Bubbles c. Blossom d. villain

12. When Mitch takes Twiggy home, The Powerpuff Girls are sure that Mitch will be mean to the hamster, and, boy, are they right. But when Twiggy turns into a monster, it's Mitch who's sorry! Real sorry.

a. Buttercup b. Bubbles c. Blossom d. villain

13. Each of The Powerpuff Girls has different things she likes to do as part of her "bedtime routine."

    a. Blossom b. Bubbles c. Buttercup d. villain

14. Sometimes Blossom, Buttercup, and Bubbles argue about the best way to fight a monster. But the Girls always make up–and kick monster butt!

    a. Buttercup b. Blossom c. Bubbles d. villain

15. Each of The Powerpuff Girls has a different thing that she likes to do in Ms. Keane's classroom at Pokey Oaks Kindergarten.

    a. Buttercup b. Blossom c. Bubbles d. villain

16. The Powerpuff Girls took in a stray squirrel once and named him Bullet!

    a. Buttercup b. Bubbles
    c. Blossom d. villain

17. The Powerpuff Girls fly through the clouds all the time. It's fun!

a. Buttercup b. Blossom c. Bubbles d. villain

18. Mojo tries to turn everyone into dogs twice—and The Powerpuff Girls stop him twice, too!

a. Bubbles b. Blossom c. Buttercup d. villain

19. Poor Elmer can't stop eating paste—and Buttercup has a hard time apologizing for teasing him about it. But when Elmer turns into a Paste Monster and Buttercup still won't say she's sorry for teasing him, Elmer makes things really sticky!

a. Buttercup b. Bubbles c. Blossom d. villain

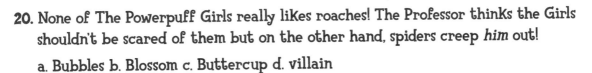

20. None of The Powerpuff Girls really likes roaches! The Professor thinks the Girls shouldn't be scared of them but on the other hand, spiders creep *him* out!

a. Bubbles b. Blossom c. Buttercup d. villain

21. One of The Powerpuff Girls' new classmates is very shy and invents an imaginary friend named Patches to keep him company. But Patches is really nasty and wrecks the classroom! The Girls have to think fast and come up with an imaginary pal to stop him!

a. Buttercup b. Bubbles c. Blossom d. villain

22. When Mojo Jojo learns that The Powerpuff Girls don't want to get near Harry because of his cooties, Mojo takes Harry along on his crimes so the Girls won't fight him. But the Girls soon learn that there's no such thing as the cooties—and that it's not so bad to get near Harry.

a. Blossom b. Bubbles c. Buttercup d. villain

23. When Big Billy decides to hang out with the Girls after they save his life, he drives them crazy by getting in their way all the time.

a. Buttercup b. Blossom c. Bubbles d. villain

24. A sleepwalking Professor steals a whole bunch of toys from the toy store. But since he was sleeping, he didn't even know he was doing it! (Plus the three Girls aren't that quick to stop him, either.)

a. Blossom b. Bubbles c. Buttercup d. villain

25. When Abra Cadaver rises from the dead and haunts Townsville with his black magic, Blossom stops him with some Powerpuff magic of her own!

a. Bubbles b. Buttercup c. Blossom d. villain

BONUS: Each of The Powerpuff Girls has her own way to fight evil, but they need them all in combo to be a successful team!

a. Blossom b. Buttercup c. Bubbles d. villain

Now that you know your mixture of sugar, spice, and everything nice, it's time to zero in on each trait by taking individual quizzes about Blossom, Buttercup, and Bubbles.

BEING A LEADER—LIKE BLOSSOM

So, as the leader of The Powerpuff Girls, I try to make sure we always have a good game plan. I like everything to be orderly and by-the-book. And on my off time, I love to work on my studies, because education is very important to me. Buttercup thinks I'm dull, but I love all the great stuff I learn. Does any of this ring a bell for you? Answer these questions the way you would respond, so you can see how much you're like me—or not!

Blossom

1. Studying conversational Chinese sounds like
- **a.** A good way to fall asleep.
- **b.** A whole lot of fun.
- **c.** A fine way to take over the world.

2. If you could have a special superpower, it would be
- **a.** Ice breath.
- **b.** Bad breath.
- **c.** Silly-string breath.

3. If you got a bad haircut, you would

   a. Tell everyone it was the new fashion and start a craze.

   b. Stay at home because you're so embarrassed.

   c. Use the haircut to help you defeat a terrible monster.

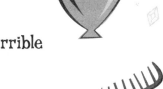

4. The best way to approach a problem is to

   a. Think about it calmly before taking action.

   b. Make a rash decision without thinking.

   c. Let other people do the thinking.

5. Helping your teacher in class is

   a. Only worthwhile if you get something good out of it.

   b. Boring.

   c. Always fun!

6. Being nice to a bad guy like Ace of the Gangreen Gang is

  a. Okay since he's so cute.

  b. Not okay, because he's a villain.

  c. A silly idea because he's a boy.

7. If an army of roaches was invading Townsville, you would

  a. Know just where to find a giant jar to trap them in.

  b. Try and stomp on them one at a time.

  c. Run screaming from the city.

8. If you made the mistake of stealing golf clubs for your dad (like I once did), you would

  a. Beg the Mayor to let you off easy.

  b. Serve your time doing community service.

  c. Fly far, far away.

9. If you had ice breath and your sisters didn't, you would

    a. Make sure not to show off your special power.

    b. Try and teach them how to get ice breath, too.

    c. Get carried away with your new power, making terrific snow cones for all the kids in school.

10. If a mysterious figure was robbing bald men of all their secrets, you would

    a. Buy all the men hats.

    b. Deduce that the mysterious figure's next victim is bound to be a very important bald man.

    c. Sit back and relax since there are only so many bald men with secret information.

ANSWERS:

Give yourself 1 point for every answer that shows you're like Blossom.

1. b. Studying other languages is a lot of fun 'cause it makes you that much smarter!

2. a. Ice breath is the coolest superpower to have. And only an icky villain or a monster would want bad breath.

3. c. When my sisters accidentally gave me a bad haircut, I was embarrassed at first, but then I used my funny looks to send an eyeball monster into a laughing fit so my sisters could defeat him.

4. a. I always think before I act, unlike Buttercup, who always acts without thinking.

5. c. I love helping Ms. Keane around the classroom.

6. b. A bad guy is a bad guy, no matter how cute he is. Buttercup had a crush on Ace of the Gangreen Gang and thought he was cute—until he tried to crush Bubbles and me!

7. a. As a leader, you have to know where to find things. When Townsville was overrun by roaches, I knew just where to find a giant jar and gather up all those roaches.

8. b. When I stole golf clubs for the Professor, I learned my lesson and did community service for Townsville.

9. c. I loved showing off with my ice breath when I found out I had it. I turned the floor into a skating rink, and I made snow cones and all kinds of other stuff. But Bubbles's and Buttercup's feelings were hurt when they discovered they didn't have ice breath like me. I apologized to them for showing off and now I only use the power when it's really necessary.

10. b. When a villain named the Robbing Leach was stealing bald men's secrets, I figured out that his next victim had to be another man who was both bald and had important information.

If you got:

10 points, you're a natural-born leader—just like me!

7-9 points, you've got a lot of strong leadership qualities in you!

3-6 points, you've got some leader stuff, but you've also got other fun features!

0-2 points, it's time to see if you're more like one of my sisters; move on to the next quiz!

ARE YOU BUTTERCUP TOUGH?

Hey! This is Buttercup! Out of us three Girls, I'm the toughest, without a doubt. Unlike Blossom, I'm into more action and less words. And unlike Bubbles, I'm not into sweet, baby stuff like flowers and sunshine. For me, being a hero is the best because you get to take on tough guys, maul monsters, and pummel punks. So, answer these questions and let's see if you've got what it takes to be Buttercup tough. *Buttercup*

1. Your favorite food for bad guys is

    a. An ice cream sandwich.

    b. A baloney sandwich.

    c. A knuckle sandwich.

2. After a good fight, you like to

    a. Stay nice and stinky.

    b. Wash your hands.

    c. Take a hot bath.

3. You like to call that dumb ol' Mojo

    a. Cutie pie.

    b. Mojoke.

    c. Mr. Jojo.

4. If Bubbles had to wear glasses,
you would

    a. Laugh your head off.

    b. Think she looked really smart with glasses.

    c. Steal them from her so she couldn't fight.

5. Kissing boys is

    a. Gross.

    b. Okay.

    c. Fun.

6. If you were insecure about your fighting ability you would

    a. Sing a special song.

    b. Rub your blanket.

    c. Say "I am mighty, mighty," five times.

7. Ace of the Gangreen Gang is

    a. Kinda cute.

    b. Gross and greasy.

    c. Dreamy.

8. If you could play with Blossom's hair, you'd make it into a

    a. Bunny.

    b. French twist.

    c. Racetrack.

9. When the Boogie Man comes to Townsville, it's time for you to

    a. Get some beauty sleep.

    b. Get a snack.

    c. Get down and boogie.

10. When you come home from school, you like to

    a. Draw flowers.

    b. Write letters.

    c. Throw punches at your punching bag.

ANSWERS:

Give yourself 1 point for every answer that shows you're like Buttercup.

1. c. A good knuckle sandwich is the best meal for bad guys!

2. a. Staying stinky is much more fun than taking baths all the time. But once I did have to clean up my act, 'cause I was so dirty that even the monsters wouldn't fight me anymore!

3. b. That dumb old Mojo deserves to be called Mojoke, since it's a joke that he thinks he can defeat us!

4. a. I totally laughed when Bubbles got glasses, which wasn't very nice, but hey, I ended up fixing her eyes with my laser vision.

5. a. Kissing boys is totally gross! When Mojo Jojo created the super-powered boy villains The Rowdyruff Boys, we had to kiss them to destroy them. Yuck!

6. b. There was a time when I had to rub my special blankie for luck before every fight or I couldn't fight well. But then I realized that I didn't need to do that to have power—I was powerful all on my own!

7. a. b. and c. Well, he is kinda cute. But then he's also gross and greasy. And I used to think he was dreamy, but then he tried to hurt my sisters—so I stopped liking him really fast! (Any one of these answers gets you 1 point.)

8. c. I "styled" Blossom's long hair into a supercool racetrack with loops and curves. You'd be amazed what that Blossom's hair can do!

9. c. When the Boogie Man blocked out the sun with his evil disco ball, he made it so everyone could party from night into day. I had a great time boogying down until we realized that the Boogie Man wanted to make it nighttime forever and terrorize the citizens of Townsville. That's when we had to shoot down the disco ball and bring the sunshine back, saving the day!

10. c. Throwing punches is a good way to stay in shape!

If you got:

10 points, you're just like me—tough as nails!

7-9 points, you're good and tough!

3-6 points, you're a little soft, but still a little tough.

0-2 points, you're more sweet like Bubbles. Move on to check your sweetness (or Bubbles) level.

A SPOONFUL OF SUGAR—THE BUBBLES WAY

Hi! I'm Bubbles and this is my quiz! Everyone's always talking about how I'm the sweet one of the group. And it's true! I like bunnies and sunshine and laughing and rainbows. I get sad when anyone gets hurt—except for bad guys. That's where my sweetness ends and I give bad guys just what they deserve—a punch in the nose! So, answer these questions and see if you are sugary sweet like me! Have fun!

Bubbles

1. When it's time to color, you

    a. Pick up your crayons.

    b. Look for some glue instead.

    c. Melt your crayons.

2. At the end of the day, you

    a. Think of your next plot to destroy the world.

    b. Read a good book.

    c. Tell your favorite stuffed animal about your adventures.

3. If Mojo kidnapped you, you would

    a. Show him you're hard-core and take his ray beam at maximum intensity: setting number 11!

      b. Hope that your sisters save you soon.

        c. Think he was a cute, misunderstood monkey and stay where you are.

          4. When it's time for fun, you like to

        a. Run through the pretty flowers.

        b. Get out your punching bag and work up a sweat.

        c. Cook up a fabulous dinner.

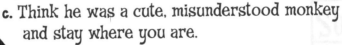

5. When it's dark, you

   a. Put on your boogie shoes.

   b. Like to leave the hall light on.

   c. Turn the lights on low and listen to relaxing music.

6. On your day off, you

   a. Put on your workout gear and do aerobics.

   b. Watch your favorite cartoon.

   c. Sit in your office, wondering where everyone is, 'cause you don't realize it's Saturday.

7. Your favorite color(s) is (are)

   a. Green, 'cause it's the color of money.

   b. Black and blue.

   c. Every beautiful color in the rainbow.

8. When you're feeling happy, you

   a. Play your banjo.
   b. Sing a pretty song.
   c. Work on your next science experiment.

9. If a monster was about to squish some ladybugs, you would
   a. Tell the ladybugs to fly away, even if you might get squished instead.
   b. Let those pesky ladybugs fend for themselves.
   c. Start a ladybug collection.

10. If you could dress up like a action hero, you would want to look
   a. Big and muscular, like Major Man.
   b. Super-brainy with lots of gadgets, like Power Prof.
   c. Powerful but cute, like a super bunny.

ANSWERS:

Give yourself 1 point for every answer that shows that you're sugary sweet like Bubbles!

1. a. I love to color with my crayons.

2. c. I like to talk to Octi, my stuffed octopus, about my day.

3. a. I showed Mojo I was hard-core and could take his nasty ray beam without crying. Now he knows not to mess with me!

4. a. I love pretty flowers! I draw them all the time!

5. b. If you're like me, you like to keep the hall light on at night. But don't worry, you can still be hard-core!

6. b. Cartoons are great. My favorite show is *TV Puppet Pals*. Mitch and Clem are the TV Puppet Pals and they tell funny jokes and hit each other with the "bonk" stick. It always makes me laugh.

7. c. I like blue and pink and orange and yellow and green and purple and every other color of the rainbow!

8. b. Singing a song when you're happy makes other people happy, too. When the nasty Mr. Mime stole all the colors from Townsville, everyone was very sad. Then my sisters and I sang a song, and everyone was happy again, and all the colors came back!

9. a. I always try to save ladybugs from getting squished.

10. c. Once my sisters and I decided to wear costumes to fight crime, and I dressed up as Harmony Bunny. It was lots of fun, but then I realized that I don't have to dress up in a costume to be a great hero!

If you got:

10 points, you're sugar-cane sweet, just like me!

7-9 points, you've got a lot of sugar in you.

4-6 points, you've got some sugar in you, but probably have some spice and everything nice.

0-3 points, you've got just a pinch of sugar. But that means you can still be nice and sweet—when you want to!

III: What Kind of Hero Would You Like to Be?

We thought it would be really neat for you to think about what kind of superpowered hero you would like to be! Here's your chance. Write down your thoughts in this section.

Bubbles

1. As you know from The Powerpuff Girls, good heroes are made up of lots of different stuff. What qualities do you have that would make you a good hero?

_____

_____

_____

_____

_____

_____

2. Being a hero is a tough job, and you should have something fun to do when you're not fighting evil. I like to color, Blossom likes to read, and Buttercup likes to punch at her punching bag. What do you like to do?

_____

_____

_____

_____

_____

_____

3. The three of us have all kinds of superpowers, like super-strength, the ability to fly, and laser eyes. Which kind of superpower would you like to have?

_____

_____

_____

_____

_____

_____

4. Each of us Girls has her own superpower color. I'm blue, Blossom is pink, and Buttercup is green. What would your superpower color (or colors!) be?

_____

_____

_____

5. Blossom, Bubbles, and Buttercup all start with "B." If you could have a Powerpuff "B" name, what would it be?

_____

_____

_____

6. I speak squirrel, monster, and Spanish. Blossom is studying conversational Chinese. What language would you like to add to your superpowers?

_____

_____

_____

7. Happy thoughts—like rainbows and licorice and fluffy clouds—help get me through hard fights. What happy thoughts help you get through a hard day?

_____

_____

_____

_____

_____

_____

8. Buttercup's motto is "Hit first, ask questions never" (which I don't think is very nice). As a new Powerpuff Girl, what would your motto be?

_____

_____

_____

_____

_____

9. If you could have a battle cry, something that you would shout before a fight, what would it be?

_____

_____

_____

_____

_____

_____

10. Even though we're heroes, we're still kids who need role models. We have Ms. Keane and the Professor and Ms. Bellum. Who do you look up to and why?

_____

_____

_____

_____

_____

_____

11. In Townsville, we fight lots of different villains and monsters. Describe a villain or monster you would like to use your superpowers to defeat.

_____

_____

_____

_____

_____

_____

12. Make up a cool hero theme song for yourself:

_____

_____

_____

_____

_____

_____

BONUS QUESTION:

What kind of superpowered hero does your town need and why?

_____

_____

_____

_____

_____

_____

_____

_____

_____

_____

_____

_____

_____

_____

IV: What's Your Powerpuff Girl IQ?

Hey! Now it's time for some more quizzes to test how much more you know about us Girls, our friends, AND our enemies. Blossom calls it finding your "Powerpuff Girl IQ," which seems pretty educational. But really, it's just a lot of fun!

Buttercup

POWERPUFF PAL MATCH-UP

This first quiz is to find out what you know about all our friends in Townsville. Each character can be matched with three things. This way you'll know more about our friends, who make the day worth saving!

Talking Dog   The Mayor   Ms. Keane

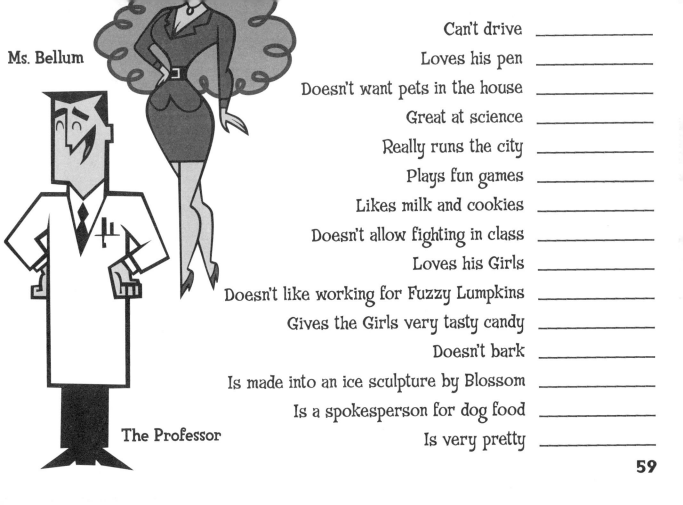

Ms. Bellum

The Professor

Can't drive _____

Loves his pen _____

Doesn't want pets in the house _____

Great at science _____

Really runs the city _____

Plays fun games _____

Likes milk and cookies _____

Doesn't allow fighting in class _____

Loves his Girls _____

Doesn't like working for Fuzzy Lumpkins _____

Gives the Girls very tasty candy _____

Doesn't bark _____

Is made into an ice sculpture by Blossom _____

Is a spokesperson for dog food _____

Is very pretty _____

59

ANSWERS:
Score one point for every correct match!

Ms. Bellum–Really runs the city, is very pretty, and doesn't like working for Fuzzy Lumpkins.

Talking Dog–Can't drive, is a spokesperson for dog food, and doesn't bark.

The Mayor–Loves his pen, likes milk and cookies, and gives the Girls very tasty candy.

The Professor–Is great at science, loves his Girls, and doesn't want pets in the house.

Ms. Keane–Plays fun games, loves the ice sculpture Blossom made of her, and doesn't allow fighting in class.

If you got:

11-15: You're a true citizen of Townsville– you really know our friends!

6-10: You know something about Townsville, but you need to visit more often!

0-5: You know as much about Townsville as the Mayor does (which isn't too much–sorry).

KNOW YOUR BAD GUYS

In order to be a powerful Powerpuff, you need to know your villains. It's an important part of saving the day. So circle each right answer and find out how much you know about these doers-of-evil.

Buttercup

1. Him tries to destroy the Girls by possessing
   a. Mojo.
   b. Octi.
   c. Buttercup.

2. Major Man becomes Townsville's new superhero by
   a. Setting up fake crimes and then solving them.
   b. Giving everyone presents.
   c. Singing a nice song.

3. Mojo turns all the people on Earth into

    a. Plants.

    b. Powerpuff Girls.

    c. Dogs.

4. A thief steals a precious diamond and hides it in

    a. A box of Happy Pappy Sappy O's.

    b. A box of Lucky Captain Rabbit King Nuggets.

    c. A box of Fruity Choco Yum Yum Crunch.

5. When the Amoeba Boys commit a crime everyone

    a. Runs in fear.

    b. Eats noodles.

    c. Pays no attention.

6. Mr. Smith is an ordinary man who just wants to be
   a. A super-genius.
   b. A super-dad.
   c. A super-villain.

7. The one thing Princess wants that she can't buy is the ability to become a real
   a. Powerpuff Girl.
   b. Stewardess.
   c. Princess.

8. The Cat hypnotizes the Professor so he can
   a. Get some catnip.
   b. Have cats take over the world.
   c. Get rid of his fleas.

9. Femme Fatale only steals

    a. One-hundred-dollar bills.

    b. Susan B. Anthony coins.

    c. Wooden nickels.

10. Roach Coach isn't really a man, he's a

    a. Roach inside a dummy.

    b. Roach inside a puppet.

    c. Roach inside a robot.

11. Mojo Jojo tries to destroy the Girls by

    a. Having monsters attack their house.

    b. Hiding their ball in his house so he can trap them.

    c. Making them drink coffee.

12. Nice Elmer Sglue turns into a
   a. Paste Monster.
   b. Mean monkey.
   c. Ice sculpture.

13. Fuzzy Lumpkins hates it when people
   a. Call him names.
   b. Leave him alone.
   c. Touch his property.

14. Lenny Baxter is the worst Powerpuff Girls fan because he
   a. Doesn't like Buttercup.
   b. Steals all the Girls' toys.
   c. Traps the Girls in plastic.

15. The Gangreen Gang destroys Townsville when they

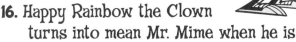

   a. Get super-villain powers.

   b. Start a boy band.

   c. Run for Mayor.

16. Happy Rainbow the Clown turns into mean Mr. Mime when he is

   a. Hit by bleach from a bleach truck.

   b. Given a new set of black-and-white clothes.

   c. Pummeled by evil crayons.

17. Sedusa tricks the Professor into grounding the Girls so she can

   a. Steal the Townsville Family Jewels.

   b. Have the Professor all to herself.

   c. Become Mayor of Townsville.

18. The Sandman puts everyone into a deep sleep so he can

   a. Steal from the Townsville Museum.

   b. Catch up on his beauty rest.

   c. Have some free time to talk to his mother.

19. The Rowdyruff Boys aren't made of sugar, spice, and everything nice. They are made of

   a. Rats, bats, and ears of cats.

   b. Logs, hogs, and the feet of frogs.

   c. Snips, snails, and puppy-dog tails.

20. When the Nanobots invade Earth, they look like

   a. Pretty flowers.

   b. Drops of rain.

   c. Rays of sunshine.

ANSWERS:

Give yourself 1 point for every correct answer.

1. b. Him possesses Octi to try and make The Powerpuff Girls fight with one another.

2. a. Major Man takes over as Townsville's superhero, until the Girls show everyone that he has been creating fake crimes to solve just to make himself look good.

3. c. Mojo thinks he can rule the world by turning everyone into dogs. He is *so* wrong!

4. b. A thief hides a huge diamond in a box of Lucky Captain Rabbit King Nuggets, but he can't stop the cereal box from leaving the factory. When he finds out that the Professor bought the Girls the cereal, the thief tries getting into the Powerpuff house to steal the cereal—and his stolen diamond—back.

5. c. The Amoeba Boys are no threat as villains, so when they commit a crime, nobody pays any attention.

6. c. Mr. Smith wants to be a super-villain, but he's really bad at it.

7. a. All Princess wants to be is a Powerpuff Girl, which is one thing money *can't* buy!

8. b. The Professor builds a ray for an evil cat that hypnotizes people into treating their cats like kings.

9. b. Femme Fatale only steals Susan B. Anthony one-dollar coins because Anthony is one of the few women on currency. (Sacajawea, the Native American guide, is also on one-dollar coins.)

10. c. Roach Coach isn't a man after all. He's really a disgusting roach inside a robot.

11. b. When The Powerpuff Girls accidentally throw their ball into Mojo's house, he tries to keep them there by hiding the ball so he can try to destroy the Girls with one of his super ray guns!

12. a. Elmer Sglue becomes a Paste Monster when he eats some nuclear glue.

13. c. Fuzzy never likes people to touch his property and goes hog-wild if anyone does.

14. c. Lenny claims to be the best Powerpuff fan, but he's really the worst because he traps the Girls in plastic for his collection.

15. a. The Gangreen Gang eat a bunch of junk food (that they've stolen) and when the Girls shoot them with their eye beams, the junk food and the eye beams join together, giving the Gangreen Gang super-villainous powers.

16. a. Rainbow the Clown turns into Mr. Mime when he is hit by a ton of bleach from a bleach truck.

17. a. Sedusa only uses the Professor to keep the Girls away so she can steal Townsville's Family Jewels.

18. b. The Sandman only wants to catch up on some beauty rest when he puts everyone to sleep.

19. c. The Rowdyruff Boys are made by Mojo out of snips, snails, and puppy-dog tails—and his own brand of Chemical X.

20. b. The Nanobots look like drops of rain, but this rain eats away at the buildings of Townsville.

If you got:

14-20 points, you know your villains well.

7-13 points, you know some of the bad boys, but not enough of them.

0-6 points, better get to know the baddies better!

And So Once Again, The Day Is Saved!

So what did you think?

How did you do?

Are you a sweetie like me?

Are you tough like me?

Or are you a leader like me? Whether you're a softy on the outside-but tough on the inside-like Bubbles, tough inside and out like Buttercup, a strong, organized leader like me, or a combo of all of us, we're sure you'd be a great Powerpuff!

We just hope you didn't identify too much with the villains, 'cause then there's going to be trouble!

74